Northern Ireland

since c.1960

BARRY DOHERTY

Heinemann Educational Publishers
Halley Court, Jordan Hill, Oxford, OX2 8EJ
a division of Reed Educational & Professional
Publishing Ltd
Heinemann is a registered trademark of Reed
Educational & Professional Publishing Ltd

OXFORD MELBOURNE AUCKLAND
JOHANNESBURG BLANTYRE GABORONE
IBADAN PORTSMOUTH NH (USA) CHICAGO

First published 2001

ISBN 0 435 32728 3
03 02 01
10 9 8 7 6 5 4 3 2 1
Designed and typeset by Jonathan Williams
Printed and bound in Spain by Edelvives
Picture research by Liz Moore

Photographic acknowledgements
The author and publisher would like to thank the
following for permission to reproduce photographs:
Camera Press / Colman Doyle: 10; Camera Press / Don
McCullin: 29; PA Photos / Stefan Rousseau: 25;
Popperfoto / Associated Newspapers: 6, 13; Popperfoto /
Reuters: 14, 16; Topham Picturepoint / Press Association:
8, 21, 23.
Cover photograph: © Popperfoto

Written sources acknowledgements
The author and publisher gratefully acknowledge the
following publications from which written sources in the
book are drawn. In some sources the wording or
sentence structure has been simplified:
*Personal Accounts from Northern Ireland's Troubles:
Public Conflict, Private Loss*, ed. Marie Smith and
Marie-Therese Fay (Pluto Press, 1999): 15B, 18F, G and
H, 19I and J; *The Sunday Times*, 1961:29A.

Dedication
For my mum and dad.

Northern Ireland since c.1960

Contents

The growth of the Civil Rights Movement

▶ **The 32 counties of Ireland.**

1. **Connaught** includes counties of Galway, Leitrim, Mayo, Roscommon and Sligo.
2. **Leinster** includes counties of Carlow, Dublin, Kildare, Kilkenny, Leix, Longford, Louth, Meath, Offaly, West Meath, Wexford and Wicklow.
3. **Munster** includes the counties of Clare, Cork, Kerry, Limerick, Tipperary and Waterford.
4. **Ulster** includes Antrim, Armagh, Cavan, Donegal, Down, Fermanagh, Londonderry, Monaghan and Tyrone. In 1920, Cavan, Donegal and Monaghan joined the Republic of Ireland.

The dotted line in the upper portion of the map represents the border between Northern Ireland and the Republic of Ireland.

Military and economic control of Ireland by English forces began in the twelfth century. This power steadily grew and, following an uprising against British rule in 1798, Ireland became an integral part of the United Kingdom in 1801. Throughout the 19th century, Irishmen began campaigning for Irish home rule and a weakening of British power. This 'Home Rule Movement' can be linked to the eventual partition of Ireland and the origin of Irish nationalism.

The Anglo-Irish Treaty of 1921 partitioned Ireland into two new countries. Throughout the 1930s both countries developed their sense of national identity in two very different directions. The Irish Free State saw itself as a largely agricultural and Roman Catholic nation. The Northern Ireland government saw itself as a modern Protestant and British state. They became very different countries with policies that deliberately set them apart from one another.

Many in the Irish Free State believed partition was a temporary measure and that unification would occur one day. However the policies introduced by the Free State's government meant that Protestants in Ulster grew to fear and even despise the character and attitudes of their southern, Catholic neighbours.

In the Irish Free State, Gaelic, not English, became the official language and a requirement for university places and entry into the civil service. Schools were forced to teach an official history of Ireland that showed the British as imperial oppressors and celebrated violent acts against British rule. The Roman Catholic Church was awarded a 'special place' in Irish society and given extensive powers in education, healthcare, government policies and censorship.

Following the actual partition of Ireland in 1922, the Northern Ireland parliament was established in a new building called Stormont Castle. It had wide-ranging powers over education, housing, local elections and policing. Northern Ireland's foreign policy, however, remained in the hands of the British government at Westminster in London. Therefore the Northern Ireland parliament had virtually unlimited control over how Northern Ireland was governed and was largely ignored by the British government until the late 1960s.

 **KEY TERMS**

Irish Free State
Ireland's name between partition in 1922 and the introduction of a new Irish constitution in 1937. Between 1937 and 1949, the country was known as Eire.

Unionist
Someone who wishes Northern Ireland to remain part of the United Kingdom. Almost all Unionists are Protestants.

Loyalist
Extreme Unionists who claim loyalty to the British Crown and the United Kingdom. Almost every Loyalist is a Protestant.

Nationalist/Republican
Someone who wants to end all ties with the United Kingdom and create a united Ireland. Almost every Nationalist is a Catholic.

The Irish Republican Army
An extreme Republican and Nationalist paramilitary organisation. Formed by Michael Collins in 1919 and active until the late 1990s.

Internment
The arrest and imprisonment of suspected terrorists without the right to charges, trial or formal investigation.

Sir James Craig, the first Prime Minister of Northern Ireland, called for a 'Protestant parliament for a Protestant people.' This was partly achieved by deliberately fixing the constituency borders to ensure Unionist victories in elections. This process (known as 'gerrymandering') ensured that leading councillors, MPs and prime ministers were always Protestant and Unionist. James Craig was determined to turn Northern Ireland into a strictly Protestant state.

The calm before the storm

In the period between 1940 and c.1968 Northern Ireland experienced a genuine period of economic prosperity and a reduction in the tension between religious and political factions ('sectarian' tension). Many factors were responsible for this:

- Despite the neutrality of the Irish Free State during the Second World War, relations with Great Britain improved. German pilots who crash landed in Ireland were kept there as prisoners until the end of the war and RAF pilots were quickly sent back to England. The RAF were also given permission to fly through Irish air space in their attempt to protect Allied shipping convoys. In 1941 fire engines and crews from Dublin were sent to Belfast following Luftwaffe air raids. Such acts of goodwill seemed to open up the prospect of better post-war relations.

- The introduction of the welfare state across the United Kingdom (which includes Northern Ireland) after the Second World War brought much needed relief and support for Catholic and Protestant families across Northern Ireland. The welfare state is the system whereby the government provides free healthcare and education. Council housing and income support were provided for those in most need, paid for through taxes.

- Unemployment benefit, maternity leave and pension benefits were increased and the creation of the National Health Service slashed the country's death rate from the highest to the lowest in the United Kingdom. In addition, 100,000 new homes were built in a slum clearance programme. Wages rose and living conditions improved faster than in most parts of the United Kingdom.

This contrasted heavily with the Republic, where there was still widespread unemployment and a high rate of emigration. Welfare support was inadequate, and the Catholic Church was condemned by the Irish media for interfering in the plans for welfare provision.

- Relations between the Irish Republic and Northern Ireland also improved during this period. The two countries co-operated in a joint campaign against the terrorist attacks of the IRA between 1956 and 1962. The success of this campaign was partly due to the decision of Brian Faulkner (later Prime Minister of Northern Ireland, 1971–74) to introduce internment.

- The Northern Ireland Prime Minister, Terence O'Neill, also attempted to bring Catholic and Protestant communities closer together. O'Neill visited Dublin in 1966 and invited two Irish Taoiseachs (the Gaelic word for Prime Minister), Sean Lemass and Jack Lynch, to Northern Ireland. O'Neill also earned the gratitude of the Catholics for allowing the Union Jack to be flown at half-mast when Pope Pius XII and later Pope John XXIII died. This was a symbolic gesture that brought respect from Catholic communities. However these actions also began to divide the Unionists, who felt that such actions threatened Protestant and Unionist power in Northern Ireland.

The Civil Rights Movement

By the late 1960s economic recession began to affect the entire United Kingdom – and Northern Ireland in particular. Traditional Northern Irish industries like shipbuilding, linen production and agriculture were badly affected and unemployment rose three times higher than unemployment on the British mainland. Slum clearance programmes stopped. The sense of post-war optimism had begun to disappear.

In the midst of growing discontent a group of middle-class Catholics met and formed the 'Northern Ireland Civil Rights Association' (NICRA) in February 1967. NICRA's members were usually Catholic and campaigned for equality in housing, employment and education between Catholics and Protestants. This peaceful organisation was inspired by Martin Luther King's civil rights campaigns which had been growing across the USA since the mid-1950s. One Nationalist described NICRA as 'middle-aged, middle-class and middle of the road'. Despite this, NICRA was met with fear and suspicion by hard-line Protestants and Unionists.

NICRA's key grievances were:

- The Ulster Unionist Party had successfully dominated national and local government in Northern Ireland since partition in 1921. Unionists defended this situation by pointing out that, since they outnumbered Nationalists in Northern Ireland, they were democratically entitled to majority rule. Nevertheless, this brought accusations that Northern Ireland was a one party state and undemocratic.

- NICRA accused the Northern Ireland government of gerrymandering – fixing constituency borders to ensure favourable elections results (for the government). In Londonderry for example, 40 per cent of

SOURCE A

Posters:
200,000 FLOOR NO VOTE in local Elect They were BRIT WHY NOT HE
One HOUSE One MAN One JOB.
JOBS ON ME EVERY SHOULD A JOB
POLICE

▲ Civil rights marchers in Londonderry, January 1969.

local government seats went to Nationalist parties, yet 60 per cent of the population there were Roman Catholic.

- Roman Catholics formed 35 to 40 per cent of the population in Northern Ireland, but just 14.5 per cent of all officers in Northern Ireland's police force, the Royal Ulster Constabulary, were Roman Catholic.

- Protestants predominantly held civil service, government and local government posts in Northern Ireland. In Belfast for instance, 97.5 per cent of council employees were Protestants.

- Catholics believed council houses were unfairly allotted to Protestant families rather than allocated on the basis of need. This also affected the voting system as homeowners and tenants had more votes.

- NICRA also objected to what it saw as the preferential treatment of Protestants in employment. Of the 111 government contracts to build factories in the post-war period only 16 had been built in Catholic areas. In addition, jobs in shipbuilding were perceived as Protestant-only careers.

Growing Protestant fears and anger

Many Protestants believed that NICRA ignored the poverty and hardship of ordinary working-class Protestants whose lives were as difficult as those of their Catholic neighbours (see Source D). Suspicions grew amongst Unionist leaders and ordinary Protestants that the movement was simply a front for Nationalists, Catholics and the IRA (see Source E).

One of the most outspoken Unionists, the Reverend Ian Paisley, was able to exploit a traditional fear and suspicion of Catholics

SOURCE B

I joined the civil rights marches because it was obvious that some people were being treated better than others. We used to accept bad housing and bad jobs. Most of my friends just went to England and didn't bother looking for work here. I had never voted and neither had my parents, brothers or sisters. There was no point, you couldn't really change anything . . . The marches awoke a sense of injustice in me and a determination to be treated equally.

A Catholic resident from Londonderry, speaking in 1999.

amongst Protestants. He formed the Free Presbyterian Church in 1951 and leads the Democratic Unionist Party which remains dedicated to maintaining Northern Ireland as an integral part of the United Kingdom. He and other extremists considered the Catholic faith satanic, and consistently described successive popes as the 'anti-Christ'. Roman Catholics were generally looked upon as being loyal primarily to the pope in Rome rather than to the United Kingdom. This meant that they were depicted as potentially untrustworthy traitors intent on uniting the Republic and Northern Ireland into one Catholic state. Unionist leaders claimed Catholics wanted 'Rome Rule' and played upon the general fear and distrust of Catholic people amongst Protestants. The special position of the Roman Catholic Church in the Irish Republic did little to disperse those fears.

The mistrust between the Catholics and the Protestants was fuelled by the way they both used history to justify their attitudes and traditions. Events such as the plantations (a scheme organised by the Tudors and Stuarts that displaced Catholic landowners and

▲ Reverend Ian Paisley campaigns for Protestant Unionism, February 1969.

replaced them with Protestant settlers from Scotland), Cromwell's invasion, the Battle of the Boyne or the great famine were used to show one or the other as cruel or unjust. Protestants were shown as foreign usurpers whose ancestors had stolen Irish land. Catholics were portrayed as lazy and untrustworthy traitors who would use terrorism to achieve a united Ireland. Both attitudes were equally simplistic and misleading.

The civil rights movement in Northern Ireland did not set out to ignite sectarian divisions and nationalism across Northern Ireland. Nevertheless by 1969 this is precisely what happened.

SOURCE E

The civil rights people don't believe in civil rights at all, they're just a bunch of republican rebels, that's what they are. Let's be very clear about this, they have no time for law and order, they have no time for this country and they mean to destroy this country, and we mean to see that this country will not be destroyed.

Ian Paisley speaking in January 1969.

SOURCE D

It was all 'the Catholics this and the Catholics that', (with them) living in poverty and us lording it over them. People looked around and said, 'What, are they talking about – us? With the damp running down the walls and our houses not fit to live in.'

A Protestant housewife, speaking in 1969.

The beginning of the Troubles

The 'Troubles' is the name given to the periods of civil unrest, terrorism and riots which took place in Northern Ireland from 1968.

Austin Currie's sit-in protest – June 1968

Austin Currie was a Catholic and Nationalist civil rights campaigner. He led a sit-in protest at a council house in County Tyrone which had recently been awarded to a single Protestant woman called Emily Beattie. Currie and fellow protestors were outraged that the house was not given to a Catholic family with children. Currie was primarily concerned with drawing attention to the way houses were allocated, but the incident suggested that the civil rights movement was always targeting Protestants and only ever concerned with Catholic interests.

Craigavon Bridge – October 1968

On 5 October 1968 a civil rights march was planned in Londonderry, to protest against what was seen as the unfair allocation of council housing. Most of the marchers were Catholic and some were believed to be members of the IRA. Despite a ban on the march entering Londonderry city centre, the organisers went ahead in an attempt to sustain the growing worldwide interest in Northern Ireland.

As the marchers approached Craigavon Bridge, in the centre of Londonderry, they were confronted by Royal Ulster Constabulary (RUC) officers. BBC Northern Ireland broadcast censored images of the protesters being pushed back by water cannon. RTE, the Irish Republic's national TV station, broadcast uncensored images of RUC officers assaulting unarmed protestors whilst innocent bystanders were attacked with water cannon. This was not long after similar scenes of police brutality in the USA – against Martin Luther King and civil rights protesters. Television viewers in Ireland and Great Britain were angered by the violent methods used by the RUC.

The incident seriously damaged the Catholics' respect for the RUC. Within Catholic communities the RUC increasingly came to be seen as the brutal and oppressive tool of the Unionist government.

A month after the Craigavon Bridge incident, following intense pressure from the British Prime Minister Harold Wilson, the Northern Ireland Prime Minister Terence O'Neill introduced reforms aimed at appeasing the civil rights protesters. The reforms of 22 November 1968 were intended to stop gerrymandering, to award council housing on need, and to begin considering reforms of votes for homeowners and tenants. However, this was too little too late, and the reforms were unable to prevent further confrontations and a major increase of violence in January 1969.

Burntollet Bridge – January 1969

On 1 January 1969 a radical offshoot of NICRA, known as 'People's Democracy' led a march from Belfast to Londonderry. It called for fairer council house distribution, more jobs and an end to extra votes for wealthier citizens. Some NICRA members were against the march because it went through strongly Protestant areas. On 4 January the marchers were seven miles from Londonderry and began crossing the Burntollet Bridge. At that point a Loyalist mob armed with sticks, stones and bottles began attacking the unarmed marchers.

Television cameras caught the RUC making very little attempt to protect the marchers. Not a single Loyalist was arrested whilst RUC officers took 80 People's Democracy marchers away. Television pictures and an official government report confirmed the attendance of off-duty B-Specials amongst the mob. B-Specials were part-time auxiliary policemen (largely Protestant) under the command of the RUC, who were allowed to carry arms and who were hated by the Catholics.

The Burntollet Bridge incident and its aftermath left the Catholic community feeling isolated and unprotected. Many Catholics began calling for their own protective force or vigilantes against RUC and B-Special oppression. It was in this atmosphere that the IRA re-emerged as a major force in Northern Ireland.

The Battle of the Bogside – August 1969

Tension increased across Northern Ireland throughout the spring and summer of 1969, particularly when the Protestant marching season began in June. Marching is a Protestant tradition dating back to 1795 which commemorates the triumph of Protestant William of Orange over Catholic King James II in 1690. The season culminates in the 12 July celebration of William's victory at the Battle of the Boyne. Another tradition is the march every August of the Apprentice Boys, a ten-thousand-strong Protestant organisation which commemorates the defence of Londonderry against the forces of King James II in 1690.

SOURCE A

▲ **Bogsiders group behind a barricade during the Battle of the Bogside, August 1969.**

On 12 August 1969 the Apprentice Boys marched along the Londonderry city walls that overlooked the Catholic Bogside area below. Bogsiders had feared attacks from these Protestant marchers and had erected barricades to prevent entry by Loyalist mobs or the RUC. A minority of Apprentice Boy marchers threw pennies at the Bogsiders, and rioting broke out between Catholics and Protestants. By the late afternoon the RUC decided to try and remove the Bogsider's barricades. Why they wanted to do this is unclear. A minority of extremist Bogsiders, perhaps remembering the Burntollet Bridge incident, began petrol-bombing the RUC.

Two days of fierce rioting followed in what became known as the 'Battle of the Bogside'. In all eight died and 750 people were injured. 270 houses were either demolished or required major repairs. In addition 1800 families were forced out of their homes as housing estates became increasingly divided. Once more the RUC and the B-Specials were discredited; television cameras recorded collaboration between the B-Specials and Loyalist mobs. Violence soon erupted across Northern Ireland, with riots in Belfast, Newry, Strabane and Coalisland.

The arrival of the British Army – August 1969

Northern Ireland appeared to be on the brink of civil war. As a result the British government in London ordered British soldiers to help the government restore law and order on the streets of Northern Ireland. At first the troops were welcomed by Catholics who famously made them tea, sandwiches and even attended army discos. They were relieved to be protected against the Protestant attacks. The army received a hostile welcome from Protestants, however.

The British government had considered sending in troops for a number of years and had placed large numbers of soldiers in nearby barracks on standby since April 1969. After the previous two years of growing conflict, and the persistent calls of Catholic residents for protection, the army entered Londonderry and then Belfast on 14 and 15 August. The precise reasons why the armed forces were sent in remain unclear.

- The official reason was to protect the Catholic population against Loyalist attacks. At first Catholics welcomed British troops as impartial or neutral peace–keepers.

- Privately the British government was aware that the number of disturbances across Northern Ireland was so great that the 3000-strong RUC could not cope any longer.

- British secret intelligence wrongly believed the IRA (see pages 14-19) was about to launch an uprising in Belfast and Londonderry. In fact the IRA lacked arms, membership and popular support at this time.

Whatever the intention behind the army's deployment – to defend the RUC, to protect the Catholics, or both – it did not prevent the army from being drawn into the violent conflict within a year.

By the end of 1969 entire Catholic communities in Northern Ireland had lost faith in the RUC and the Northern Ireland government. The Civil Rights Movement had given way to enormous discontent and open hatred of British rule. It was in this atmosphere of anger, fear and insecurity that the IRA emerged as the unofficial guardians of the Catholic communities against the RUC, the Loyalist mobs and, later, the British army.

The Falls Road curfew – July 1970

The army's potential to act as a neutral, and therefore impartial, peacekeeping force was shattered when the new Conservative government at Westminster gave the Northern Ireland government at Stormont powers to direct army operations. The Catholic communities then perceived the army as a tool of the Unionist government. In an incident known locally as 'The Rape of the Falls', 3000 British soldiers, acting on out-dated information and orders from Stormont, searched the Catholic Falls Road (in Belfast) for guns, explosives and ammunition. In a non-stop 35 hour ordeal between 3 and 5 July, the Falls Road residents were placed under an army curfew whilst houses were searched, floorboards ripped up, and innocent men and women arrested on suspicion of terrorism. Tear gas was fired at angry residents. During the curfew four people died, one crushed by an army vehicle, and there were seventy-five other casualties.

In a single week the army lost its reputation as a neutral peace-keeping force and destroyed the goodwill it had created in the previous twelve months. Now it became a target for angry Nationalists.

Internment – August 1971

Support for the IRA increased even further with the introduction of internment on 9 August 1971. Internment led to the immediate arrest and imprisonment of 340 Catholics without charges, a trial or formal investigation. In addition some of those interned were subjected to 'experimental interrogation techniques' that involved sleep, food and water deprivation in an attempt to disorientate the prisoner. This had an impact on relations between Catholics and the government.

Despite dozens of murders carried out by Loyalist gangs and the intimidation of Catholic communities, not a single Protestant was interned at this stage. Again, this gave Catholics the impression that the Northern Ireland government was acting only in the interests of the Protestant communities. It was seven months before the first Protestants were interned. By February 1972 nearly 2500 people had been interned in this way. Most of these people were eventually released because the arrests had been based on out-of-date or inaccurate RUC secret intelligence reports, for example, not a single IRA leader was arrested. This period of internment was, unlike ten years earlier, unsuccessful in preventing terrorist violence.

Bloody Sunday – January 1972

On Sunday 30 January 1972, a 15,000 strong crowd marched through the streets of Londonderry protesting against the continuation of internment. The march was to go to the Guildhall through the Catholic Bogside area. Since internment all marches had been made illegal. The army wanted to contain the marchers in the Bogside and prevent them reaching the Guildhall, and so put up a number of barriers. As the crowd of marchers reached the barriers, the Parachute Regiment, apparently in the belief that it was under fire, opened fire on the crowd. The result was 14 deaths and 13 injured.

One of the most lasting images from the tragedy came from Father Edward Daly, a Catholic priest from Londonderry. Television cameras caught his attempt in vain to remove a fatally wounded seventeen-year-old boy from the scene by waving a white handkerchief at soldiers who fired on the crowd. Later, Father Daly told of how he watched the boy get shot (see Source C).

▲ Father Daly waves a white handkerchief at soldiers on Bloody Sunday.

SOURCE C

He suddenly gasped and threw his hands in the air and fell on his face. He asked me: 'Am I going to die?' and I said 'No', but I administered the last rites. I can remember him holding my hand and squeezing it … I knelt beside him and told him, 'Look son, we've got to get you out', but he was dead. He was very youthful looking, just in his seventeenth year but he only looked twelve.

Father Daly describes the death of a young victim of Bloody Sunday.

In their defence the Parachute Regiment claimed they had been fired on first by gunmen amongst the protesters, who were also preparing to throw nail bombs. However, the army suffered no injuries and no nail bombs or guns were recovered from the scene.

The official British enquiry into the deaths, led by Lord Widgery, infuriated Catholics when it was published. It upheld the army's claim that IRA gunmen in or around the crowd had fired first. However, the Widgery Report also condemned the soldiers' actions as 'bordering on the reckless'. Angry Catholics dismissed the Report as a 'whitewash' and further evidence of an unjust and prejudiced government. The introduction of internment and the events of Bloody Sunday encouraged even greater recruitment and support for the IRA.

The introduction of Direct Rule – March 1972

Northern Ireland's new Prime Minister, Brian Faulkner, believed internment would destroy the IRA as it had in the early 1960s. In fact internment further aggravated the violence and left Northern Ireland in a permanent state of crisis. The British Prime Minister, Edward Heath, became increasingly frustrated as Brian Faulkner and Stormont failed to reduce violence or introduce elements of power-sharing that involved Catholics.

Finally, on 24 March 1972, Stormont's powers were suspended and Direct Rule was introduced from Westminster in London. The suspension of Stormont's powers to govern Northern Ireland brought to an end over 50 years of self-rule. In its place the British government established a 'Northern Ireland Office', headed by the Secretary of State for Northern Ireland. In an atmosphere of failed internments, continued civil rights marches, sectarian violence, revenge attacks and growing international condemnation, Edward Heath planned Direct Rule as a temporary measure to prevent Northern Ireland from slipping further into chaos before a settlement could be reached. However, this 'temporary' measure was to continue for the next 25 years. The prolonged search for a settlement is detailed on pages 20–8.

The escalation of violence

The re-emergence of the IRA

SOURCE A

▲ **The devastated community centre at Enniskillen following a massive IRA bomb explosion, November 1987.**

The Irish Republican Army's roots date back to the rebellion against British rule in 1916 known as the Easter Uprising, but the IRA had been declining in both popularity and numbers up to the late 1960s. 'I Ran Away' became a popular phrase to describe the slow reaction of the IRA to protect Catholics against RUC and Loyalist attacks on civil rights marches and homes.

In 1970 the IRA split into two groups, the 'Official' IRA and the 'Provisional' IRA. The 'Officials' wanted a united Ireland. The 'Provos', based in Northern Ireland, also wanted a united Ireland, but believed that the only way to end British occupation was to use violence. The IRA's impact in Northern Ireland

started slowly throughout the winter of 1970, as hundreds of volunteers to the Provisional IRA were trained in guerrilla warfare, ideology and anti-interrogation methods. The IRA's recruits were largely working-class youths from Londonderry, Belfast, Armagh, Tyrone and Down.

Support for the IRA amongst Catholic communities in Northern Ireland grew rapidly following Bloody Sunday. The USA's enormous Irish-American population donated millions of dollars to organisations like NORAID, that were merely a front for the IRA. In addition, the IRA received weapons, training and money from Libya, the Palestinian Liberation Organisation and Basque

> *Well, I've had thirteen punishment beatings by paramilitaries: iron bars, sledge-hammers and hurley bats ... If you got caught by the police you were taken to court. And when the courts were done with you, they [the paramilitaries] were after you, so you were getting done two ways.*
>
> **Reported by an anonymous Londonderry resident.**

separatists in Spain. This allowed the IRA to become possibly the most powerful terrorist organisation in the late twentieth century.

Before internment the IRA's campaigns against the British were fairly disorganised and unplanned, consisting usually of crude petrol-bombing or stone-throwing. Following internment in August 1971, the IRA had become more organised and targeted the RUC and British Army with shooting and bombing campaigns. The change in tactics resulted in a massive increase in IRA killings; the IRA were responsible for two deaths in 1969, 18 in 1970, 86 in 1971, and 235 in 1972.

The IRA hoped to create so much chaos and destruction in Northern Ireland that the state would become ungovernable. They believed this would force a solution to the crisis, and in September 1971 the solution the IRA demanded was a united Ireland with complete independence from British rule.

In Northern Ireland itself the IRA also acted as an unofficial police force within Catholic communities. Drug dealers, pimps, protection racketeers, thieves and other criminals were often reported to the IRA rather than the RUC (see Source B). The IRA punished such alleged criminals using a variety of methods. These included punishment beatings,

kneecapping, tarring and feathering, shaving women's hair, and forced exile or execution.

Loyalist paramilitaries

The first killings in what became known as the 'Troubles' were carried out by Loyalist paramilitaries. The paramilitaries were organisations of both Nationalists and Loyalists who were prepared to use violence to achieve their aims. In response to the wave of Nationalist celebrations commemorating the fiftieth anniversary of the 1916 Easter Uprising, the Ulster Volunteer Force (UVF) was revived. By the year 2000 over 550 people had died at the hands of the UVF, particularly in the years between 1971 and 1975.

Loyalist paramilitaries were dedicated to maintaining Northern Ireland as an integral part of the United Kingdom. They believed that they belonged to a long Protestant tradition of resistance against Catholic ambitions. Loyalists often claimed their origins as far back as 1690 when the Apprentice Boys of Londonderry resisted an invasion by the Catholic King James II.

By 1971 the Ulster Defence Association (sometimes known as the 'Ulster Freedom Fighters') had also been formed. Both the UDA and the UVF believed that internment, the RUC and the army, had all failed to stem the rise in IRA attacks. Therefore both were originally formed as vigilante style groups aimed at protecting Protestant communities.

Both the UDA and the UVF were openly sectarian in their attacks. They targeted Catholics in retaliation against the IRA. This triggered a cycle of violence that saw innocent Protestants and Catholics dragged into conflict. The most notorious of these Loyalist paramilitaries were the 'Shankhill Butchers' (see Source F on page 18). In 1979, 11 members of the gang were found guilty of 19 deaths and sentenced to a total of over 2000 years in prison.

▲ The bloody interior of O'Toole's bar where 6 people died after Loyalist gunmen opened fire, June 1994.

During the early 1990s the numbers killed by Loyalist paramilitaries began to exceed those killed by the IRA. This led the IRA to make several failed attempts to kill the Loyalist paramilitary leaders. In one instance, an IRA bomb carried by one of its members, Thomas Begley, unexpectedly blew up in a fish and chip shop on the Shankhill Road. Leaders of the UDA were due to meet in a room above the shop later that day. Nine people, including Begley, were blown up in the explosion. Later in the same month, UDA gunmen retaliated by entering a Catholic bar in Greysteel and killing seven people. This tit-for-tat cycle of violence was typical for the period of almost thirty years from 1970.

SOURCE D

Responsibility for deaths

Republicans / Nationalists (e.g. IRA, INLA, Real IRA)	2145
Loyalists (e.g. UVF, UDA, Red Hand)	1061
Security Forces (e.g. British Army, RUC, UDR)	365
Other	80

The scale of suffering across the British Isles

The map and Sources D – L are intended to give an indication of the level of suffering experienced across the British Isles throughout the 'Troubles'. Statistics are based on figures of those killed up to the end of the year 2000.

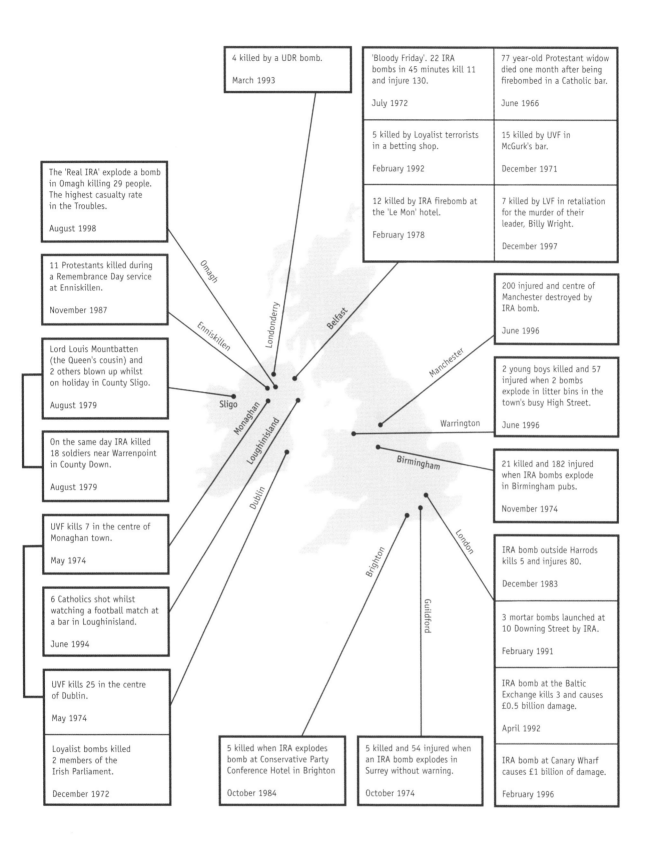

4 killed by a UDR bomb.

March 1993

'Bloody Friday'. 22 IRA bombs in 45 minutes kill 11 and injure 130.

July 1972

77 year-old Protestant widow died one month after being firebombed in a Catholic bar.

June 1966

5 killed by Loyalist terrorists in a betting shop.

February 1992

15 killed by UVF in McGurk's bar.

December 1971

12 killed by IRA firebomb at the 'Le Mon' hotel.

February 1978

7 killed by LVF in retaliation for the murder of their leader, Billy Wright.

December 1997

The 'Real IRA' explode a bomb in Omagh killing 29 people. The highest casualty rate in the Troubles.

August 1998

11 Protestants killed during a Remembrance Day service at Enniskillen.

November 1987

Lord Louis Mountbatten (the Queen's cousin) and 2 others blown up whilst on holiday in County Sligo.

August 1979

On the same day IRA killed 18 soldiers near Warrenpoint in County Down.

August 1979

UVF kills 7 in the centre of Monaghan town.

May 1974

6 Catholics shot whilst watching a football match at a bar in Loughinisland.

June 1994

UVF kills 25 in the centre of Dublin.

May 1974

Loyalist bombs killed 2 members of the Irish Parliament.

December 1972

200 injured and centre of Manchester destroyed by IRA bomb.

June 1996

2 young boys killed and 57 injured when 2 bombs explode in litter bins in the town's busy High Street.

June 1996

21 killed and 182 injured when IRA bombs explode in Birmingham pubs.

November 1974

IRA bomb outside Harrods kills 5 and injures 80.

December 1983

3 mortar bombs launched at 10 Downing Street by IRA.

February 1991

IRA bomb at the Baltic Exchange kills 3 and causes £0.5 billion damage.

April 1992

IRA bomb at Canary Wharf causes £1 billion of damage.

February 1996

5 killed when IRA explodes bomb at Conservative Party Conference Hotel in Brighton

October 1984

5 killed and 54 injured when an IRA bomb explodes in Surrey without warning.

October 1974

Omagh

Enniskillen

Londonderry

Belfast

Sligo

Monaghan

Loughinisland

Dublin

Manchester

Warrington

Birmingham

Brighton

Guildford

London

▲ A history of the Troubles, 1966–98.

SOURCE E

Status of deaths

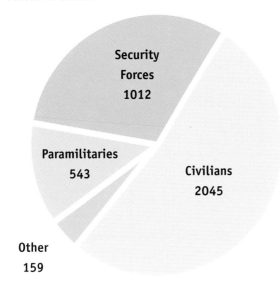

Security Forces 1012

Paramilitaries 543

Civilians 2045

Other 159

SOURCE G

My brother wasn't really mutilated too badly. He'd lost his legs and his arm and half his head. But the other lad was absolutely in bits and pieces. And I thought it was very cruel. Because when they went to identify the bodies, the policeman or whatever threw a black bag up on the table and says, 'Identify your son!' My daddy was able to identify my brother because compared to the other two he wasn't really that badly mutilated. I thought that was the cruellest of things to do. And my daddy couldn't get over it. He used to disappear every night and when he came back from his pigeon shed you could see he'd been crying.

Written by Alice Nocher, a Catholic resident in North Belfast. Her brother and his friend were both killed by a Loyalist bomb explosion in 1975.

SOURCE F

We stood with the body about fifteen minutes. There wasn't many words exchanged. My older brother, he was just devastated, he couldn't even talk. You couldn't put it into words. I was looking at this thing. It resembled a piece of beef that had been beat with hatchets and hammers and stabbed, and fingers missing and nose stitched back on the face, head caved in, throat cut right back to the spinal cord. I was taking all these details in. You probably go through your whole life and never see a sight like that.

Paul Morrissey describes how he and his brother identified his father's body following his father's murder by the Shankhill Butchers.

SOURCE H

I was travelling down from Andersonstown in a private car with a companion after doing a day's duty. Both him and I were clad in civilian clothes. On the West-link (motorway), a car came along as if to overtake and as it drew level with us the occupants of the passenger front seat and the passenger rear seat opened up with what I know to be an Armalite rifle and a Thompson sub-machine gun.

The experiences of an anonymous ex-RUC officer.

SOURCE I

They threw the grenade at her and blew the whole side out of her and she was killed. The other girl got it in the foot. But the girl that she told to lie down she got it in the legs. [My sister] was shot through the breasts. And when she landed on the ground she damaged her whole back.

A relative of a former prison warden describes an IRA attack on her sister and three friends.

SOURCE J

I think it was after the formation of the UDR [Ulster Defence Regiment – a part-time regiment of the British Army]. A number of ones we drank with were suddenly in the UDR, and coming home at night, getting stopped by them, and then the ridiculous thing of them asking your name, which, one night, when it first happened, turned into a laugh from ourselves in the car. But we seen fairly quickly that the ones who were asking it weren't seeing it as a laugh. I felt physically afraid of some areas or if you were stopped at night by the UDR you were very much conscious that this was like a Protestant Loyalist force.

A former member of the IRA, Lawrence McKeown, describes how old friends became new enemies.

SOURCE K

I bear no ill will. I bear no grudge. Dirty talk of that sort will not bring her back to life. She was a great wee lassie. She loved her profession. She was a pet. She's dead. She's in heaven and we'll meet again. Don't ask me, please, for a purpose … I don't have an answer … It's part of a greater plan, and God is good, and we shall meet again.

Gordon Wilson's reaction to the murder of his daughter following an IRA explosion at the Enniskillen Remembrance Service in 1987.

SOURCE L

How would you like British soldiers looking through your sister's bedroom window from their watchtowers? Everyone knows they have heat-seeking cameras that can look through curtains and windows. They watch us and they watched her. Sometimes when we walked past the soldiers, they would make comments or whistle at my sister. In the end no one slept in that room.

A young Catholic student explains why he feels sympathy for the IRA attacks on the British Army.

The search for a settlement in the 1970s and 80s

The impact of Direct Rule

Over 50 years of self-rule had come to an end when the power of Stormont to govern Northern Ireland was removed in 1972 (see page 13). The 'Northern Ireland Office', headed by the secretary of state for Northern Ireland, was intended as a temporary and preventative measure against further trouble, or even civil war, in Northern Ireland. Throughout the next 25 years each successive Northern Ireland secretary attempted to reach a settlement and restore peace across the province. The first attempt began in 1973.

The power-sharing executive and the Sunningdale Agreement – 1973

William Whitelaw, the first Secretary of State for Northern Ireland under Direct Rule, gathered representatives from the Nationalist and Unionist parties to a conference in Sunningdale, Berkshire. Whitelaw wanted to reassure Unionists by promising that Northern Ireland would remain a part of the UK as long as the majority of the Northern Irish people wished. He hoped to appease the Nationalists by giving them some control over major decisions in Northern Ireland and allowing the Republic of Ireland a small say in the running of the country.

Following weeks of tense discussions, the Sunningdale Agreement was signed on 9 December 1973. The terms of the Agreement were:

- Major decisions would be agreed by a Northern Ireland 'power-sharing executive' that gave both the Nationalists and the Unionists a say in the running of the country.

- A Council of Ireland would be created that brought together representatives from the Republic of Ireland and Northern Ireland. They would regularly meet to discuss any issues of concern and to agree on appropriate action.

The Agreement was greeted with much hope and optimism amongst moderate Nationalists in Britain and across Ireland. Unionists were united in their rejection of any agreement that was to lead to joint government with Catholics and the Republic of Ireland. The IRA maintained that any agreement that stopped short of a united Ireland and the withdrawal of all government from England was totally unacceptable.

In the early months of 1974, Brian Faulkner (leader of the Ulster Unionist Party) became increasingly isolated and unpopular amongst fellow Unionist politicians and voters because of his apparent support for the Sunningdale Agreement. Unionists became frightened that the Agreement was the first step to a united Ireland and many simply could not agree to any sharing of power with Catholics. Elections in February 1974 revealed Unionist voters were against the Agreement by a majority of three to one.

In May 1974, increasing hatred of both the power-sharing executive and the Council of Ireland amongst the Unionist communities led to a general strike, lasting two weeks. The strike, organised by the Protestant Ulster Workers Council, resulted in road blocks, demonstrations and power cuts across Northern Ireland. The strike began with little support and might have ended quickly, if it hadn't been for the intervention of the Ulster Defence Association who actively encouraged, and even pressurised, workers to join the strike. However, by 27 May, with most of Northern Ireland at a standstill, Brian Faulkner and the entire power-sharing executive resigned. Direct Rule from London was reintroduced and the search for a peaceful settlement continued.

Sinn Fein and the hunger strikes

Sinn Fein is commonly regarded as the political wing and 'voice' of the IRA. In a top secret IRA document known as the 'Staff Report', the IRA claimed they controlled Sinn Fein and ordered members to 'agitate around social and economic issues which attack the welfare of the people.' Sinn Fein's role was to

win support for the IRA amongst all Catholics, and Catholics in Northern Ireland in particular. Sinn Fein's leaders consistently deny that they are also the leaders of the IRA, but many of their political opponents in Northern Ireland claim that the two organisations are one and the same.

In the 1970s Sinn Fein did not take part in any elections. Both Sinn Fein and the IRA did not believe the British government would cut its ties with Northern Ireland through agreement. They believed that only violence would force the British to withdraw (see Source B for the views of one IRA member). However, in the early 1980s Sinn Fein began to change this strategy by entering local and national elections for the first time. This major decision to enter politics in an attempt to bring about a united Ireland followed a series of hunger strikes amongst IRA prisoners.

SOURCE A

▲ Protestors in support of those on hunger strike, April 1981.

On 1 March 1976 all newly convicted paramilitaries lost their 'special category status'. This meant that they were no longer classified as political prisoners, but as ordinary criminals. This change in status meant that new IRA prisoners were no longer permitted to wear their own clothing, refuse prison work or associate freely within their prison block. In addition, visiting rights and parcels became restricted.

Against the wishes of its leadership, IRA prisoners began to refuse to wear prison clothing and instead wore only their prison-issue blanket. By 1978, some 300 IRA prisoners were 'on the blanket'. However, public support or interest in the blanket protest was minimal. Therefore IRA prisoners began a 'no wash' protest that meant prisoners refused to wash, shave, brush teeth or empty their slop buckets each morning. It was at this point that prisoners embarked on the most unpleasant stage of the campaign with the 'dirty protest'. IRA prisoners daubed their own excrement on their prison walls in a strategy that successfully attracted worldwide horror and ultimately sympathy. The prison authorities responded with forced showers, shaves and haircuts, and the cells were disinfected. The IRA went further by embarking on a murder campaign against prison warders that resulted in the deaths of 19 warders between 1976 and 1980.

By 1980 the 'dirty protest', or the 'battle of the bowels' as it became known, had begun to lose momentum and instead IRA prisoners began hunger strikes in an attempt to regain special category status. The first wave of hunger strikes was led by Brendan Hughes in 1979, but failed to alter British policy.

By the end of January 1980, Bobby Sands, leader of all IRA prisoners at Long Kesh Prison, called for a second hunger strike. IRA prisoners were unhappy that their demands for special category status had still not been met. On 1 March 1980 Bobby Sands was the first of ten prisoners to go on hunger strike. One month into his hunger strike, Bobby Sands stood as an independent MP in the Fermanagh and South Tyrone by-election, winning a seat in Westminster convincingly. Sinn Fein and the IRA were certain that Margaret Thatcher would not allow a fellow MP to die. Another hunger striker, Kieran Doherty, stood for and won a County Cavan seat in the Dublin parliament. On 5 May Bobby Sands was the first to die, 66 days into his hunger strike. 100,000 mourners lined the route of his funeral procession.

On 3 October 1981, the last of the ten hunger strikers finally died, after 217 days. The strikes had failed to shift British policy on prisoner status. However, there was now an increased wave of support and sympathy for both the IRA and Sinn Fein, not just within Ireland, but across the world. The public sympathy created by the hunger strikes was not lost on Sinn Fein (led by Gerry Adams), which in the following years set about challenging the Social and Democratic Labour Party (SDLP) as the main Nationalist political party in Northern Ireland. The SDLP has consistently condemned the use of violence, and now Sinn Fein and the IRA began moving towards a belief that a solution could be achieved through political agreement rather than through terrorist campaigns.

 **SOURCE B**

Our aim is to create such psychological damage to the Brits that they'll withdraw. Sick of the expense, the hassle, the coffins coming back to England.

Quoted from a member of the IRA known only as 'Pat'.

SOURCE C

▲ Gerry Adams at a Sinn Fein press conference, May 1983.

For five years, Sinn Fein looked like toppling the SDLP as the central voice of Irish Nationalism, especially in Northern Ireland. In the 1983 British general election, Gerry Adams won the West Belfast constituency from Gerry Fitt, the leader of the SDLP. Across Northern Ireland, Sinn Fein won 13.4 per cent of the vote. However, by 1987 a mixture of continued IRA atrocities and the 1985 Anglo Irish Agreement resulted in a decline in support for Sinn Fein. Nevertheless, the hunger strikes brought Sinn Fein into a peace process that was to bear fruit in the next decade.

The Anglo Irish Agreement - 1985

Between 1980 and 1985 Prime Minister Margaret Thatcher met with Irish Taoiseachs Charles Haughey and later Garrett Fitzgerald. Both countries wanted to find a way to end sectarian violence and establish a peaceful and lasting solution.

The eventual Anglo Irish Agreement signified a step forward in the search for peace because the British government began to consider the need for a greater involvement of the Irish government in Northern Ireland's affairs.

- Both countries would develop closer co-operation to improve security, share information about terrorist activities, and develop laws that were held in common – especially to enable easier exchange of prisoners.

- Regular inter-governmental conferences were set up between the Secretary of State for Northern Ireland and the Irish Foreign Affairs Minister.

- The Irish government accepted the legitimacy of the State of Northern Ireland – but only as long as its people consented to it.

- The British government accepted the possibility of a united Ireland – but only if the majority consented to such a change.

The Agreement was generally welcomed in the Irish Republic, the British mainland and in the USA. However, reactions in Northern Ireland were very mixed indeed. Of all the political parties, only moderate Nationalists like the SDLP and the Alliance Party, which appealed to both Catholics and Protestants, showed their approval of the Agreement. Sinn Fein condemned the Agreement because it effectively accepted the partition of Ireland.

Northern Ireland Unionists were united in their outrage at the Agreement. All of Northern Ireland's 15 Unionist MPs withdrew from the House of Commons and encouraged workers' strikes and mass protests. They believed that the Agreement was a step nearer to a united Ireland. At one point, in November 1985, these protests appeared to threaten the future of the Anglo Irish Agreement when over 100,000 Unionists gathered outside Belfast City Hall. But within two years the protests had died down, after Margaret Thatcher continually refused to break the Agreement.

Whilst the Anglo Irish Agreement was a first significant step in the peace process, it did not bring about a lasting settlement in Northern Ireland. The Dublin and London governments became increasingly divided and publicly critical of one another. London became frustrated with Dublin's refusal to extradite (hand over) wanted IRA suspects, and privately wanted more co-operation in joint anti-terrorist operations. The Dublin government continually criticised Britain for apparent miscarriages of justice involving those accused of outrages, as occurred after the Birmingham and Guildford bombings in particular.

The search for a settlement in the 1990s

The Downing Street Declaration

Between 1989 and 1993 representatives from all of Northern Ireland's main political parties began discussing with the British and Irish governments possible solutions to end hostilities. The peace process appeared to be gathering momentum.

Discussions between the British Prime Minister John Major and Irish Taoiseach Albert Reynolds resulted in their issuing the 'Downing Street Declaration' on 15 December 1993. The document stated three major agreements:

- Both London and Dublin agreed that 'it is for the people of Ireland alone, by agreement between the two parties respectively, to exercise their right of self-determination on the basis of consent, freely and concurrently given, North and South, to bring about a united Ireland, if that is their wish'.

- Both governments agreed to give 'full respect for the rights and identities of both traditions of Ireland.'

- Cross-party talks would be set up – but only those parties that condemned violence would be permitted to join.

Moderate Nationalists welcomed the declaration because it seemed that the British government accepted the possibility of a united Ireland. But this apparent shift in British policy worried the Unionists because the British government no longer appeared determined to keep Northern Ireland as a part of the United Kingdom.

In the following months, Albert Reynolds put pressure on Sinn Fein to renounce violence and seek a democratic and political settlement to the conflict. When Gerry Adams visited the USA in February 1994 he was treated as a celebrity, but the support he received from Bill Clinton, Teddy Kennedy and other leading politicians was dependent on Sinn Fein pursuing peaceful, rather than violent, policies.

▲ British Prime Minister John Major (left) and Irish Taoiseach Albert Reynolds issuing the 'Downing Street Declaration', December 1993.

It appears that Sinn Fein and the IRA may have sensed that the political atmosphere in Ireland, Britain and the USA had changed and that the time had come to concentrate on peaceful negotiations. In April a secret IRA publication – the 'Totally Un-Armed Strategy' (TUAS) – was distributed among active members. This hinted that the IRA might consider non-violent methods in the pursuit of its aims to achieve a united Ireland. On 31 August 1994, the IRA declared a ceasefire.

In October 1994, Loyalist paramilitaries also declared a ceasefire. They also offered an apology, giving 'the loved ones of all innocent victims over the past 25 years abject and true remorse'. Then, on 9 December, Sinn Fein began the first formal talks in 22 years with representatives of the British government.

The ceasefire ends

Throughout the 17 months after the IRA ceasefire began, many Nationalists became frustrated with the British government's apparent lack of pace. John Major remained committed to finding a peaceful settlement, but was at the same time suspicious of both the permanence of the IRA ceasefire and Sinn Fein's ultimate political demands.

Although the IRA had halted their shooting and bombing campaigns, they remained an unofficial police force within Catholic communities in Northern Ireland. Catholic youths continued to be beaten up or exiled if found guilty of alleged crimes within the Nationalist community. These so–called 'punishment beatings' were seen by both Unionists and John Major as evidence of the IRA's lack of commitment to peace.

The year 1995 had the lowest death rate (nine) since 1968, but tension remained between Nationalist and Loyalist communities and was particularly apparent during the marching season. In July the RUC escorted a parade of Orangemen through a Catholic district at Drumcree near Portadown in County Armagh. These Orangemen were members of the 'Orange Order' founded in 1795, dedicated to upholding Unionist traditions and heritage. Nationalists across Ireland were furious at this decision.

Further progress with the peace process negotiations was stalled by the IRA's refusal to decommission (hand over) their weapons. Despite the intervention of US Senator George Mitchell, who was perceived as being an outstanding peacemaker and negotiator, a compromise could not be reached. As a result the IRA ended their ceasefire by exploding a bomb near the Canary Wharf building in London in February 1996. The bomb claimed two lives, caused one billion pounds worth of damage, and left a very uncertain future for the peace process. The IRA continued its bombing campaign and in June 1996 destroyed the centre of Manchester in an explosion that injured 200 people.

The May 1997 general election saw the Labour Party come to power under Tony Blair. The government immediately set about breathing life into the peace process. The following month Blair reopened talks with Sinn Fein and announced all-party talks in September. Sinn Fein were invited to attend the talks on the condition that the IRA called a ceasefire, which it did in July. Cross-party talks were therefore resumed in the autumn, despite the refusal of Ian Paisley's Democratic Unionist Party (DUP) to enter into talks that involved Sinn Fein.

The Good Friday Agreement

In March 1998 Senator George Mitchell declared that the 'time for discussion is over' and that it was 'time for a decision'. He set the deadline of 9 April 1998 for all parties to reach agreement on the future of Northern Ireland. As the deadline approached, all night discussions took place involving all parties and, eventually, Tony Blair and Irish Taoiseach Bertie Ahern. Then finally, at 5.36 pm on Saturday 10 April, Senator Mitchell announced the contents of the Good Friday Agreement between the British government, the Dublin government and the main Northern Ireland political parties, including Sinn Fein (which had now renounced violence):

- The state of Northern Ireland was legitimate and would remain a part of the United Kingdom unless the majority of the Northern Irish people voted otherwise.

- The Irish Republic would end its claim to be the rightful government of Northern Ireland.

- A new 'Northern Ireland Assembly' would take over control from Westminster of education, health, agriculture and law-making.

- The Assembly would have 108 members appointed by proportional representation, to guarantee a full representation from all communities.

- The Assembly would have ten separate ministries with their own committees. Both the ministers and the committees would be appointed according to party strength.

- A 'Council of the Isles' would be formed with representatives from Ireland, Northern Ireland, Scotland and Wales. Their role would be to act as a consultative body.

- Human rights and equality would be guaranteed.

- All political prisoners would be released within two years if their associated paramilitary organisation maintained their ceasefire.

- Former Conservative MP, Chris Patten, a Catholic, would head a 'Policing Commission' to examine the future of the Royal Ulster Constabulary.

- All parties agreed to use their influence to bring about decommissioning of weapons within two years.

The Agreement was met with intense media interest and worldwide relief. John Hume, the leader of the SDLP, and David Trimble, leader of the Ulster Unionist Party, were later awarded the Nobel Peace Prize for their determination to reach a positive conclusion. Elements within the Unionist community, particularly Ian Paisley's DUP, flatly condemned the Agreement, claiming that the government was 'selling out to terrorists'.

Events moved very quickly after the Agreement was announced. In May a referendum, by which the people are asked to vote directly on a key issue, was held in both Northern Ireland and the Republic of Ireland to ratify the Agreement. The Agreement received a 94 per cent backing in the Republic and a 71 per cent backing in Northern Ireland. The Agreement was safe, although Unionists as a whole appeared only slightly in favour of the Agreement. In June, elections were held to the Northern Ireland Assembly and were won convincingly by pro-Agreement parties. David Trimble became its First Minister, and Seamus Mallon (of the SDLP) became his deputy.

Northern Ireland since the Good Friday Agreement

Problems with hard line Loyalists and Nationalists and the decommissioning of weapons still needed to be resolved. However, it was the issue of the marching seasons that was to provide the first challenge.

As 12 July 1998 approached, Orangemen gathered in the small town of Drumcree planning to march down the Catholic Garvaghy Road, which had been their usual route for generations. Another violent face off between the protesters and the RUC spilled over into widespread disturbances across Northern Ireland. Both sides stood firm and bloodshed seemed inevitable. Then, on 12 July, a Loyalist bomb killed three boys in County Antrim. The deaths of such innocents, combined with the fact that one parent was Catholic and the other Protestant, created such shock that the Orangemen called off their parade out of respect. Worse was to follow in August when the hardline paramilitary group that calls itself the 'Real' IRA exploded a bomb in Omagh, killing 24 people who had been shopping that afternoon (see Source B).

 **SOURCE B**

The dead, all civilians, consisted of Protestants, Catholics and two Spanish visitors, and included young, old and middle-aged, fathers, mothers, sons, daughters and grandmothers. Unborn twins also died.

From a book written by David McKittrick and David McVea, *Making Sense of the Troubles.*

The two bombings only helped to make politicians in Northern Ireland even more determined to make the Agreement work.

The issue of decommissioning

It was not until 2 December 1998 that the Northern Ireland Assembly met for the first time. The continuation of punishment beatings and the failure of the IRA to decommission weapons had slowed down the process considerably. In November 1998, Senator Mitchell had helped to draft a proposal that initiated decommissioning after the Northern Ireland Assembly met for the first time.

The pressure on both Sinn Fein and the IRA mounted when Mitchell said any failure to decommission would 'leave this society uncertain and vulnerable'. The Ulster Unionist Party eventually agreed to the proposal with David Trimble adding, 'We have done our bit, Mr Adams, it is over to you. We have jumped, you follow'.

Between 11 February and 5 June 1999 the Northern Ireland Assembly was temporarily suspended. Power returned to the new Secretary of State, Peter Mandelson, after the UUP grew tired of waiting for any progress on IRA decommissioning. Following a statement by the IRA that they would begin 'a process that will completely and verifiably put the IRA arms beyond use' and permit neutral inspectors to regularly monitor their arms dumps, David Trimble and the UUP agreed to return to the Northern Ireland Assembly.

On 19 January 1999 the Patten Report was published. It recommended sweeping changes to the name, uniform, symbols and royal references of the RUC. In addition, Patten recommended minimum quotas of Roman Catholics within the force, and an independent and representative committee to monitor Northern Ireland's future police force. The Report was rejected by the Northern Ireland Assembly on 25 January and remains an unresolved issue.

The future of Northern Ireland

The future of the Northern Ireland Assembly hangs in the balance and largely depends on the issue of weapons decommissioning. On 30 May 2001 (two years after the Good Friday Agreement), neutral observers confirmed that the IRA had not attempted to remove weapons from their arms dumps and therefore were keeping to their ceasefire agreement. However, many Unionists are still not satisfied as they have not yet seen evidence of a single decommissioned weapon.

Whilst the general ceasefire has held since 1998, peace and normality in Northern Ireland are threatened by the existence of splinter groups. The key paramilitary groups, like the IRA, UVF and UDA, all eventually agreed to a ceasefire. However, some of their own supporters refused to accept the decision and created their own rival organisations. The IRA, for instance, split into the 'Continuity IRA' and the 'Real IRA'.

Most observers agree that the future of Northern Ireland depends on whether a sustained period of economic, political and social stability can be maintained. It is hoped that the people of Northern Ireland will stop voting along strictly sectarian lines and begin voting on 'ordinary' issues like healthcare, social security, pensions and education. Only then will Northern Ireland experience an extended period of normality and turn its back on violence forever.

Sample coursework assignment

SOURCE A

From an article in the *Sunday Times* newspaper in 1961.

The big employers were privately run companies and although Catholics regularly suspected anti-Catholic prejudice among foremen or personnel managers, it is a hard thing to prove. All that can be recorded is that of 10,000 workers in a Belfast shipyard – the biggest single source of employment in the city – just 400 were Catholics.

Fermanagh County Council itself employed 370 people: 322 of the posts, including the top ones, were filled by Protestants. Within the Education Authority the most sought-after jobs were bus drivers, because of the long rest and holidays. Of about 75 school bus drivers in Fermanagh, all but seven were Protestant. The population of Fermanagh was more than half Catholic.

SOURCE B

Billy Sinclair, a former player-manager of Linfield, a football club in Northern Ireland, talking in 1984.

If you're a Linfield scout and you see a lad who's good, the second or third question is, 'What school did you go to son?' And if it's Saint something, then all of sudden the boy isn't good enough. He kicks with the wrong foot.

SOURCE C

From a document published by Ulster Protestant Action, an organisation formed in 1959 by the Reverend Ian Paisley and other Unionists.

Keep Protestants and loyal workers in employment in times of depression in preference to their fellow Catholic workers.

SOURCE D

▲ Photograph of the house of a Catholic family, taken in Londonderry in the 1960s.

SOURCE E

Results of local elections in Londonderry in 1966.

	Nationalist Votes	Unionist Votes	Nationalist Councillors	Unionist Councillors
South Ward	10,047	1,138	8	0
North Ward	2,530	3,946	0	8
Waterside	1,852	3,697	0	4
Totals	14,429	8,781	8	12

SOURCE F

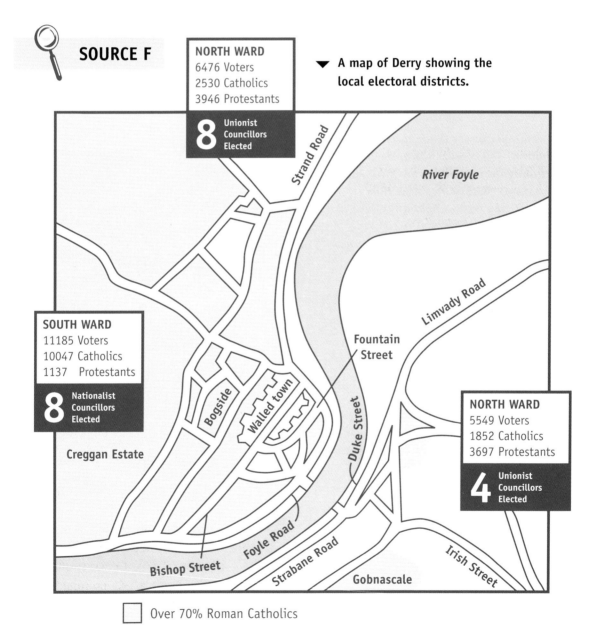

NORTH WARD
6476 Voters
2530 Catholics
3946 Protestants

8 Unionist Councillors Elected

▼ A map of Derry showing the local electoral districts.

Strand Road

River Foyle

Limvady Road

Fountain Street

SOUTH WARD
11185 Voters
10047 Catholics
1137 Protestants

8 Nationalist Councillors Elected

Creggan Estate

Bogside

Walled town

Duke Street

NORTH WARD
5549 Voters
1852 Catholics
3697 Protestants

4 Unionist Councillors Elected

Bishop Street

Foyle Road

Strabane Road

Gobnascale

Irish Street

☐ Over 70% Roman Catholics

SOURCE G

The Reverend Ian Paisley
speaking on a television programme
broadcast in Britain.

*Interviewer: Who was behind civil
rights in your view?*

*Paisley: The Irish Republican
              Army, or at that time
              those who were dedicated
              to the views and objectives
              of that army.*

SOURCE I

From a report on the Northern Ireland
Civil Rights Association produced for the
British Government in the early 1970s.

*The membership was politically varied
and undoubtedly included persons of
known extreme Republican views and
activities as well as members of the
Northern Ireland and Liberal Parties.
In addition, the membership is mostly
Roman Catholic. It is and always had
been a basic rule of the association to
place no bar on people from political
groups. There is no doubt that the IRA
has taken a close interest in the Civil
Rights Association from its beginning.*

*It is undoubtedly the case that it has
been the policy of the Association to
refuse to permit the display of
provocative symbols and banners, in
particular the Republican tricolour,
at any demonstration that it has
organised.*

SOURCE H

Michael Farrell, a member of the
Northern Ireland Civil Rights Association,
speaking on the same television
programme as the Reverend Ian Paisley.

*There were a number of Republicans
and the proportion of them varied
from time to time, but they never
dominated it. They were never in
control, at least not until maybe later
on. They were also used as stewards
on civil rights marches, but the
stewards always played the role of
trying to prevent trouble, in fact the
younger People's Democracy often had
clashes with the stewards because we
felt that the stewards were
co-operating too much with the police.*

▲ A cartoon drawn in 1991 by Martyn Turner, a
Northern Irish political cartoonist. It was
used to illustrate the front cover of a book
called *Troubled Times*, about the Troubles in
Northern Ireland from 1970 to 1991.

❓ Assignment One: Objective 1

1. Describe the disadvantages faced by the Catholics in Northern Ireland in the mid-1960s. (15)

2. How did Protestant politicians explain the social, economic and political differences between Catholic and Protestant? (15)

3. Why were British troops sent to Northern Ireland in August 1969? (20)

(Total: 50 marks)

❓ Assignment Two: Objectives 2 and 3

1. Study Source A. What can you learn from Source A about the disadvantages faced by Catholics in Northern Ireland in the early 1960s? (6)

2. Study Sources B and C. How useful are these sources in helping to assess the extent of discrimination against Catholics? (10)

3. Study Sources D, E and F. All of these sources refer to a single city in Northern Ireland. Use the sources, and your own knowledge, to explain why this city became a centre of the Civil Rights Movement in Northern Ireland. (12)

4. Study Sources G, H and I. Do Sources H and I support Reverend Ian Paisley's view of the Civil Rights Movement given in Source G? Explain your answer by reference to all three sources. (8)

5. Study Source J. Do you agree with this portrayal of the reasons why the Troubles continued into the 1990s? Explain your answer using the sources and your own knowledge. (14)

(Total: 50 marks)